G

Little book of

Easter

Words of hope, joy and new
beginnings

RICHARD DALY

WILLIAM
COLLINS

William Collins
An Imprint of HarperCollins*Publishers*
77–85 Fulham Palace Road
London W6 8JB

www.williamcollinsbooks.com

1 3 5 7 9 10 8 6 4 2

First published in Great Britain in
2011 by HarperCollins*Publishers*
This edition 2013

A catalogue record for this book is
available from the British Library

ISBN 978-0-00-751386-4

Printed and bound in China by
South China Printing Co. Ltd.

Introduction

Easter marks the time for new beginnings
and the imagery of Easter is all about new
life and growth. That's exactly what happened
on that resurrection morning – Christ came
forth from the tomb alive having conquered
sin and death, giving us the perfect
gift of eternal life.

This little volume is designed to bring you
hope and renewed strength as you journey
through the various pathways of life with
all its challenges, griefs and fears. Open
this book at any page and you will find a
reflection inspired by Scripture to bring you
comfort and assurance and remind you
that you are not alone.

Jesus Christ, who suffered, died and is now alive, wants you to claim his many promises of strength for your life.

May you be inspired by the hope that comes with the meaning of Easter.

Richard Daly

Abide in him

'He is not here, he is risen!' is probably the greatest announcement ever made in the history of the world. Let these words assure you that your God is not only alive and well, but lives within your heart.

For Further Reflection

Luke 24:5, 6

Make a change

Easter brings with it a message of hope,
promise and a new start for your life.
Let this occasion be an opportunity for
a new you to come alive.

For Further Reflection
2 Corinthians 5:17

You are priceless!

At the cross we discover our true value;
for it is there that we discover the price
God was willing to pay for us.

For Further Reflection

1 Corinthians 6:20

The greatest gift

The greatest gift is giving at the greatest
cost to the least deserving. That's what God
did when he gave us Jesus Christ.

Look beyond the cross

When you have a purpose in life, you will be less affected by the obstacles that come your way. Instead of hindrances, they become stepping stones to success.

For Further Reflection
Philippians 3:13, 14

You're worth dying for

Everything God made was very good: that
means you too. Endeavour to see yourself
as God sees you; he wants to change your
self-image so you can appreciate your
unique gifts and qualities.

For Further Reflection

Genesis 1:31

He overcame – you can too

Remember, God is not bound by
circumstances, and neither is he overcome
by our problems. In every situation he has
the power to provide a way out for you.
Put your trust in him.

For Further Reflection
Psalm 121:1–3

Arise to a new hope

Ultimate peace begins when we have peace with God. Regardless of your past, your future is still untapped. He is willing to forgive and forget – just ask him.

For Further Reflection
1 John 1:9

Be restored

Broken relationships can often lead to
broken hearts. God promises to heal the
broken-hearted. Not only does
he heal, he also restores.

For Further Reflection

Psalm 147:3

Take Jesus at his word

Jesus said that in three days he would
rise again. His promises never fail –
every one of them is like a precious
jewel just waiting to be discovered.

For Further Reflection
2 Peter 3:9

Seek your destiny

God did not create or redeem you to live a purposeless existence. He has a customised plan just for you. Seek it, find it, live it to the full.

For Further Reflection
Romans 12:6

Give and you will receive

Think of all that Christ has done for you –
then share one of these special moments
with someone who needs encouragement.
Whatever comfort they receive will
rebound on you.

For Further Reflection
Luke 6:38

Call him up

Through prayer you can live in continuous contact with God. Be encouraged – you will always have someone on your side.

_____

For Further Reflection
1 John 2:1

Know where you're going

The worst kind of life is one without
purpose – with Christ you get a purpose
and a plan to go with it.

For Further Reflection

Jeremiah 29:11

Grow into your dreams

Remember dreams always come a size
too big, so you can grow into them.
Don't settle for mediocrity.

For Further Reflection
Mark 9:23

Hold his hand

Today you are not alone – God is with you. He says, 'I will never leave you, nor forsake you.'

For Further Reflection

Hebrews 13:5

Believe in a big God

God wants you to stretch your faith a little further. If you want to experience a miracle you have to step out in faith!

_____

For Further Reflection
Matthew 9:29

Keep focused

You don't have to let fear limit your
vision when God is your source, because
his supply is unlimited.

For Further Reflection

Philippians 4:19

Expect a miracle

Just one idea from God, just one, can
change your life and the lives of others.
He's got great things in store for
you today – expect them!

For Further Reflection
Isaiah 55:9

Keep your head up

Life can become humdrum and wear you
down. Instead of going around complaining,
put a smile on your face – your altitude
changes your attitude.

For Further Reflection

Philippians 4:1

Know your friends

Solomon said, 'A friend loveth at all times,'
not just when you comply with their
wishes. Jesus is a friend who sticks
closer than a brother.

For Further Reflection

Proverbs 17:17

You are precious

Jesus was asked if he could come down from
the cross and save himself. Aren't you glad
that he sought to save you instead?

For Further Reflection
Luke 19:10

The greatest substitute

Jesus took our punishment so the Father
could embrace us. Now we have a brand new
relationship with our Father through grace.
Isn't that amazing?

For Further Reflection

Matthew 8:17

Be courageous

Taking a new step is what we fear most, yet our real fear should be standing still. Step forward into growth and development.

For Further Reflection

Joshua 1:7–9

Waste no time

Time is an equal opportunities employer.
We all get 24 hours, 1440 minutes, 86,400
seconds daily and we must account for
how we use them.

_____

For Further Reflection

Psalm 90:12

One day at a time

Worry doesn't rid tomorrow of its challenges,
it robs today of its joy. Remember, God gives
you today's strength for today's needs.

For Further Reflection
1 Peter 5:7

Claim your breakthrough

Breaking the habit of a lifetime isn't easy.
It requires an act of real faith and asking God
for the courage to follow through.

For Further Reflection
Revelation 21:7

God knows what he's doing

God doesn't waste anything. He'll use all of
your experiences – the good, the bad and the
ugly – to prepare you for your next challenge.

For Further Reflection

Romans 8:28

Power in the blood

Easter says you can put truth in a grave,
but it won't stay there.

C. W. Hall

For Further Reflection
John 8:32

You're never forgotten

Jesus will never forget you. You are
graven on the palms of his hands.

For Further Reflection
Isaiah 49:16

New every year

Easter is a promise God gives to each
of us, and the promise of a new
life starts in him.

For Further Reflection
Lamentations 3:23

From death to life

Christ bore our sins in his body on the cross,
but he died as a victorious saviour. He died as
our saviour but now lives as our Lord.

For Further Reflection

Revelation 1:8

Christ makes you
a new person

The resurrection of Jesus Christ from
the dead changes everything – your past,
your present and your future.

For Further Reflection

2 Corinthians 5:17

God gives you more than you ask

We have been forgiven, redeemed and reconciled to God our heavenly Father. It's a three-in-one salvation package.

For Further Reflection

Matthew 7:7, 8

Stay cool

Your attitude is like a thermostat –
it determines the climate. If you want to
control your climate, control your attitude.

For Further Reflection

Philippians 3:21

Your help is assured

Jesus came not to be served but to serve.
His mission was that of a suffering, humble
servant. He turned the whole concept
of a lord upside down.

For Further Reflection
Matthew 20:28

Choose life

God wants us to be happy and joyful.
One way this can be achieved is when we
walk straight along the path the Lord
has set before us.

For Further Reflection

Deuteronomy 30:19

He is with you

Whatever you are facing today, Jesus
knows how you feel. He is fully acquainted
with all our sorrows.

For Further Reflection
Isaiah 53:3, 4

Draw near to God

Victory comes when you draw closer to
the one who defeated the tempter both in
life and in death. So call on him today.

For Further Reflection
Jeremiah 33:3

Release your potential

Jesus knows the worst about you, yet he
believes the best in you. He sees you not as
you are, but as you will be when he
gets through to you.

For Further Reflection

1 Samuel 16:7

Keep climbing

Sometimes it might seem that the mountain
is too high and we're tempted to give up.
That's when we need to listen to his voice:
'Have not I commanded you? Be strong
and courageous.'

For Further Reflection

James 1:12

The battle is not yours

You will never win if you fight in your own strength; so don't even go there. God's already given you authority over all the power that the enemy possesses and nothing shall harm you.

For Further Reflection

Luke 10:19
1 Samuel 17:4, 7

Chosen from the beginning

What God told Jeremiah is true of you:
'Before I made you in your mother's womb,
I chose you, before you were born
I set you apart.'

For Further Reflection
Jeremiah 1:5

Jesus never fails

Having conquered death and the cross,
Christ's next mission is to return, this time
not as a suffering lamb but as King of
kings and Lord of lords.

For Further Reflection

Psalm 136:3

Don't let go

If you feel scared, you will find total security
when you hold on to the hand of Jesus.
He will never let go of his grip.

For Further Reflection

Psalm 48:10
Psalm 73:23

You're bought with a price

Your future is not in the hands of people,
it is in the hands of God. And what he
owns he takes care of.

For Further Reflection
Isaiah 4:1

Don't settle for second best

The truth is your accomplishments may bring you some joy, but only in God's presence will you find fullness of joy.

_____

For Further Reflection

Psalm 16:11

Claim your eternal home

To the repentant thief on the cross Christ's words were: 'Today you shall be with me in paradise.' It's a promise that speaks to you – claim your paradise today.

For Further Reflection
John 14:1–3

You're loved beyond measure

To the chanting mob the dying Christ said:
'Father, forgive them, for they know not
what they do.' Even in his suffering, he still
reached out to cover the sins of his accusers.
What selfless love!

For Further Reflection
Jeremiah 31:3

Don't despair

Our God, who is 'the beginning and the
end', sees things in their completed state,
including your ultimate victory.

For Further Reflection

Revelation 22:13

Your formula for success

For every battle God has a strategy. Don't just
pray about the battle – ask God to show
you the plan for victory.

For Further Reflection

Judges 6:16

If God is for you ...

Your God is greater than any opposition
you are facing!

For Further Reflection

Romans 8:31

Give praise to God

God loves to start with nothing, for then there's no doubt about who has the power and who gets the credit!

For Further Reflection

John 15:5

Be a conqueror

Life is about overcoming! When you've
conquered one mountain, before you know
it you're faced with the next – a bigger one.
Remember the battle's not yours, but God's.

For Further Reflection

1 John 4:4

Be available

Through the power of God's indwelling
Spirit you can make a difference. Just make
yourself available to God and let him show
you what he can do with your life.

For Further Reflection
Philippians 3:13, 14

Just believe

Assurance of a place in heaven comes only
through accepting Jesus as your personal
saviour, believing that he died for your sins
and rose again to give you everlasting life.
No more is needed, no less will get you in.

For Further Reflection

John 3:16

Develop an attitude of gratitude

Begin thanking God today for what he's done
and what he's going to do on your behalf,
because he will come through for you.

For Further Reflection

Psalm 92:1
Ephesians 5:20

Let God rule

Stop trying so hard to make things happen on your terms, and begin allowing God to make things happen for you on his terms.

For Further Reflection

Proverbs 3:5, 6

Don't be sidetracked

When you're doing anything worthwhile,
expect opposition from those who aren't
privy to God's plan in your life. That goes
with the job.

For Further Reflection

Proverbs 16:7

Seek godly wisdom

The decisions you make today will affect not
only you but future generations – so seek
God to make the right move.

For Further Reflection

Proverbs 4:5

Hang on in there

Just because it hasn't happened yet, this doesn't mean God has changed his mind. While you are waiting, God is still working.

For Further Reflection

James 1:4

Accept God's timing

If you're asking God to make you bigger
instead of better, you may be disappointed.
God won't give you what you're not
ready to handle.

For Further Reflection

Luke 16:10

Let him mould you

Remember you are still a work in progress –
God's not finished with you yet!

For Further Reflection

Jeremiah 18:4

Prove your love

Loving God is a commitment, an attitude
resulting in action, a focus, a daily decision
to acknowledge him in your life. So ...
do you love God?

For Further Reflection

Revelation 2:4

Cast your burdens on him

Our capacity for handling stress is limited
and preventing stress is always better than
trying to deal with it. So cast all your cares
on the Lord – he will sustain you!

For Further Reflection
Matthew 11:28, 29

Accept God's pardon

Jesus came to let you know that the penalty of sin has been removed and its power is broken. In God's eyes, you're loved and accepted!

For Further Reflection
Nehemiah 9:17

Don't be hard on yourself

If God is willing to pardon your mistakes
and even bury them, isn't it time you stopped
beating yourself up? Receive his grace
and move on!

For Further Reflection

Philippians 3:13

Don't stay down

Falling down is just a part of learning to walk.
Don't be discouraged – God is still at work in
your life, so get up and try again.

For Further Reflection

Proverbs 24:16

Think positively

Think excellent thoughts! Whatever enters
your mind repeatedly occupies, shapes and
controls it, and in the end expresses itself
in who you are and what you do.

For Further Reflection

Philippians 4:8

Build on solid ground

God's love for us is set in concrete. That's
the foundation you build your life on.

For Further Reflection

Romans 8:39

Don't be overwhelmed

God has a purpose behind every problem.
But he also has a protective shield in
front of it.

For Further Reflection

Romans 8:28
Ecclesiastes 3:17

Trust God's way

God often uses circumstances to accomplish his will. The reason is obvious: we face circumstances 24 hours a day.

For Further Reflection

1 Peter 1:7

Turn obstacles into stepping stones

Adversity draws us closer to God. There are things we learn about God when we're in trouble that we can't learn any other way. But remember, 'The Lord is close to the broken-hearted.'

For Further Reflection

Psalm 34:18

Let go

Submitting the situation to God and trusting him with the means and timing is hard for most of us to do. Why? Because it means giving up control, but remember he won't fail you!

For Further Reflection

James 4:7

Think big

Big oak trees grow from little acorns. When you discover your God-given dream and commit to it, there's no telling how far you'll go or what impact you'll make.

For Further Reflection
Matthew 21:21

Let God lead

Stop trying to control every possible outcome! Life is much more peaceful when you decide to stand on God's word and trust him, regardless of circumstances.

For Further Reflection

Proverbs 3:7

Be patient in waiting

Patience is what God gives you when bad things remain unchanged. It's faith taking its time.

For Further Reflection

Romans 5:3

Stay calm

Next time you get all worked up, ask yourself,
'What is the enemy trying to do here?'
Do your utmost to exercise self-control
and remain in peace.

For Further Reflection

Ephesians 4:27

Live to the max

Christ's desire for you is that in this world
you live your life to the full.

For Further Reflection

John 10:10

Keep your eyes on Jesus

God's message of salvation is very clear.
'Look to me and be saved ... For I am
God and there is no other.'

For Further Reflection
Isaiah 45:22

Be reunited

Atonement is the term for us being
reconciled to God through Christ's sacrifice.
It allows us to experience 'at-one-ment'
with our Lord once again.

For Further Reflection

Romans 5:11

God can handle it

The scriptures present Christ as the
sin-bearer of the human race. Now that's
a load of sins placed on his shoulders.

For Further Reflection

Isaiah 53:6–12
2 Corinthians 5:20, 21

Washed in the blood

When we come to God in repentance
he does not see us dressed in our sinful
garments. He sees Christ's robe of
righteousness covering us and we are
pronounced redeemed, cleansed and
clean in his Spirit.

For Further Reflection

Isaiah 61:10

You can do it!

Christ's life provides the assurance that we can live victoriously. You can do all things through Christ who strengthens you.

_____

For Further Reflection

Philippians 4:13

The joy of Easter

Good Friday will remain 'good' because
of what happened on Easter Sunday.

For Further Reflection
1 Corinthians 15:17

Depend on him

God will never give you an assignment
you can complete without his help, so don't
even try it alone.

For Further Reflection

2 Samuel 22:3

You are not alone

Many are the afflictions of the righteous
but the Lord delivers him out of them all.
'When you can't see him, his eyes are
always on you!'

For Further Reflection
Psalm 34:19

You've been restored

While we were distant from God, he came
down to be our friend.

For Further Reflection

Proverbs 18:24

Undeserved favour

In Christ we are not only pardoned but
acquitted and declared righteous.

For Further Reflection

Romans 5:6–10

Easter Sunday's blessing

It is nothing that we have done but
everything Christ has done that makes
us worthy.

For Further Reflection

Titus 3:5

Stay at the feet of Jesus

No matter how sinful your past life is,
how far you've strayed or how low you've
stooped – there's still room at the
cross of Jesus for you. ˙

For Further Reflection

Ephesians 1:7

Let God remake you

Only the creator who created something out of nothing can transform your life. He can take your nothing and make you something.

For Further Reflection
1 Thessalonians 5:23

Control your thoughts

Whoever occupies our mind, occupies us.
That's why God says, 'Let this mind be in
you that was in Christ Jesus.'

For Further Reflection
2 Corinthians 10:5

Resurrection hope

When Christ said those final words,
'It is finished,' it ushered in the start of
a new life for us.

For Further Reflection
1 Peter 1:23

Don't run ahead of God

God will not accelerate his pace to catch up with ours. We need to slow down in order to get back into step with him.

For Further Reflection

Psalm 46:10

Don't give up!

Endurance means staying the course.
Jesus 'endured the cross' – he completed
the course so that we can be winners.

For Further Reflection

James 1:3

Let God recreate you

God loves to take the lost, the last, the
least and the lowest and make them into
something beautiful. To him you are
the apple of his eye.

For Further Reflection

Zechariah 2:8
2 Corinthians 5:17

Expect great things
to come

Don't you know that God has more for you?
If you trust him with your future, your best
days are yet to come!

For Further Reflection

Isaiah 43:18, 19

Forgive as you have been forgiven

Practising forgiveness stems from a deep gratitude to God for wiping out a debt so great we could never have repaid it.

For Further Reflection

Luke 23:24

Trust God completely

When Jesus said to his Father, 'Into your hands I commit my spirit,' that was a cry of surrender and trust to the Father.

For Further Reflection

Luke 23:46

You've been set free

With Jesus being a ransom for us, God wrote
'Paid in full' over every sin you've committed,
from the womb to the tomb.

For Further Reflection
Colossians 2:13, 14

The future is bright

Jesus does not penalise us for our past,
locking us into it forever. Knowing the worst
about us, he still believes the best.

Bask in the love of God

Nothing can change the way God feels about you. Nothing can alter the fact that he will continue to love you regardless of what you do or say.

Let God start afresh

From the resurrection we can see that God causes dead things to come alive. What needs to come alive in your life today?

For Further Reflection

Colossians 3:1

Stay blessed

What's so amazing about grace? The fact
that you are alive right now and he's keeping
you breathing each day is amazing!

For Further Reflection

Acts 15:11
1 Corinthians 15:11

You are special

Jesus could have called 10,000 angels
but he died alone for you and me.

You're saved by grace

What makes you a Christian is not perfection, it's God's forgiveness.

For Further Reflection

Romans 5:15

Let not your heart be troubled

Easter can bring hope to a person devastated by the loss of a loved one. It brings the promise of a heavenly reunion.

For Further Reflection

John 14:1–3

Rest in his arms

The word '*Abba*' simply means 'Daddy'.
How wonderful! He simply wants us to
come to him at any time, crawl into his lap,
feel secure in his everlasting arms and
call him 'Daddy'.

For Further Reflection
Romans 8:15

You mean everything to him

If God didn't hesitate to put everything
on the line for you, is there anything else
he wouldn't gladly do for you?

For Further Reflection

Romans 8:39

Predestined to be saved

God didn't choose you because you're
a wonderful person. He chose you because
he wanted to.

For Further Reflection

Ephesians 1:5

Light of the world

When Jesus was crucified the earth
was plunged into darkness. But on Easter
morning the light came on – for ever.

For Further Reflection

2 Samuel 22:29

It's not too late

You can't do anything about your past,
but starting today you can do something
about your future – one choice and
one act at a time.

_____

For Further Reflection
Job 14:14–17

Claim his promises

Jesus is the only man ever to make an
appointment beyond the grave and show
up for it. You can be assured he always
keeps his promises.

For Further Reflection

John 11:25

Turn your mourning into dancing

Christ's resurrection guarantees ours. If you have experienced the heartache of burying those you love, Easter guarantees you'll meet them again, alive, immortal, glorified and just like Jesus!

For Further Reflection

1 Thessalonians 4:16, 17

Be content

Happiness is not about getting what you
want, it's about enjoying what you've got!
So keep your perspective and be
grateful every day.

For Further Reflection
1 Timothy 6:8

Live life intentionally

God has a plan and a destiny for your life.
Living according to his will unlocks these
pathways to eternity.

For Further Reflection

Proverbs 16:9
Proverbs 19:21

Rise and shine

Today the greatest announcement still speaks from the tomb: 'He is not here, he is risen!'

For Further Reflection

Luke 24:6

He's incredible

Sin could not overpower him, suffering could not prevent him, death could not hold him and the tomb could not contain him. Don't you want him by your side?

For Further Reflection

Jeremiah 32:27

Be washed

Would you be free from your burden
of sin? There's power in the blood,
power in the blood!

L. E. Jones

For Further Reflection
Revelation 1:5

Let him in

Today Jesus says, 'Behold I stand at
the door and knock. If anyone hears my
voice I will come in and eat with him
and he with me.'

For Further Reflection
Romans 3:20, 21

Put Christ first

Your priorities determine how you spend
your time, so set them prayerfully and
maintain them carefully.

Seek godly wisdom

Each choice is a crossroads in life, one that
will either confirm or compromise your
commitment. Let your integrity be the gauge
of the direction you choose.

For Further Reflection

John 10:27

Hold on

Nothing in my hand I bring,
simply to your cross I cling.

A. M. Toplady

For Further Reflection
1 Timothy 6:12

Be heavenward bound

The biggest fact about Joseph's tomb was
that it was not a tomb at all; it was a room
for a transient. Jesus just stopped there ...
on his way back to glory.

H. B. Smith

For Further Reflection
1 Corinthians 15:55

Jesus paid it all

He wept and mourned so we can laugh
and rejoice. He was apprehended that
we might escape. He was betrayed that
we might go free.

John Bunyan

For Further Reflection
1 Corinthians 6:20

Sealed for life

Jesus cannot forget us; we are sealed
with the promise of the Holy Spirit.

For Further Reflection
Ephesians 1:13

The ultimate sacrifice

No pain, no palm;
no thorns, no throne;
no gall, no glory;
no cross, no crown.

William Penn

For Further Reflection

Hebrews 12:2

Count your blessings

1 cross
2 thieves
3 nails
4 given

For Further Reflection
Genesis 49:25, 26

God knows all

Only God could have remembered
through the winter, cold and grey
how to renew the earth with beauty
and give us Easter day.

Helen Steiner Rice

For Further Reflection

Job 21:22

Celebrate your Easter

On Easter morn he showed he is our saviour.
His resurrection proves he is our Lord.
That is why we tell you 'Happy Easter';
he secured our heavenly reward.

Joanna Fuchs

For Further Reflection
1 Corinthians 1:18

The greatest story

The best of the story is the very last part;
It's why on Easter we're filled with pleasure.
Death could not our saviour hold;
his power is beyond all measure.

Joanna Fuchs

For Further Reflection
Matthew 1:21

Be free in Christ

Without showing mercy, life becomes
an endless cycle of resentment and
retaliation. But as you walk in love,
you experience freedom.

For Further Reflection
Colossians 3:13

Don't stay down

Regardless of how often you've been knocked down, God always offers you his almighty hand to pick you up, clean you up and give you a chance to begin again.

For Further Reflection

Psalm 51:2

Be still and know

Following Jesus can't be done at a sprint;
you can't go faster than the one who's
leading, so slow down, don't rush ahead –
spend time with him!

For Further Reflection
Matthew 11:28

You're worth it

Just think: the God of the universe willingly
left the splendour of heaven, was born
into poverty and died on a cruel cross for
wayward humanity. Why? Because that's
how much you mean to him!

For Further Reflection

Romans 6:7

You are unique!

If you were the only one in need of salvation
in the entire world, Jesus would have gone
through all that he did just for you!
What amazing love!

For Further Reflection
Romans 5:15

Let him find you

Contrary to popular opinion, God does not wait for you to come to him. God comes to seek and find you. He will never let you go.

For Further Reflection

Psalm 139:7

God's mind is made up!

There is nothing we can do to make
God love us more. There is nothing we
can do to make God love us less.

Philip Yancey

For Further Reflection

John 3:16

The suffering servant

He was wounded for our transgressions,
bruised for our iniquities; the chastisement
for our peace was upon him, and by his
stripes we are healed.

For Further Reflection
Isaiah 53:5

Protected from the enemy

When God looks at you, he sees only the one
who surrounds you! Because you're in Christ
your victory is secure. You can rejoice!

For Further Reflection

Zechariah 3:3, 4

Open your heart

It's impossible to be merciful until we've thoroughly come to terms with our own need for mercy and received it from the Lord.

For Further Reflection

Lamentations 3:22, 23

Dedicate yourself to Jesus

What you are is God's gift to you; what you
do with yourself is your gift back to him.

For Further Reflection

2 Corinthians 9:15

Seek ye first

Today, ask God to show you his priorities for
your life, and then set your personal goals
accordingly. There's no feeling like knowing
you're doing the right thing at the right time.

For Further Reflection

Matthew 6:33

Remember how he led you

With God a delay is not a denial. Remember
how far you've come, not just how far you
have to go. You may not be where you
want to be, but neither are you where
you used to be.

For Further Reflection

John 1:4

Go the extra mile

Want to experience a miracle? Then be
willing to stretch your faith a little more.
Put God to the test!

_____

For Further Reflection
Malachi 3:10

Make a change within

If there's any cross we are to carry, it is the cross of self-denial and submitting our will to the all-wise God.

For Further Reflection

Matthew 16:24

You can start again

Baptism means 'to immerse' – what a
wonderful representation of Christ's death,
burial and resurrection! We come up out of
the water and we are a new creation. The old
things have passed away, the new has come.

For Further Reflection
Romans 6:4

Be comforted

One of the titles of the Holy Spirit is
'comforter'. It means 'to be called to the side
of' – when we lose a loved one we have
the assurance from the God of all comfort
that he will be with us.

For Further Reflection
2 Corinthians 1:3, 4

Put God to the test

Ask great things and expect great things
from God. He is faithful and will fulfil
his promises.

For Further Reflection

Luke 6:38

Do what God asks

'What does the Lord require of you but to
do justice, to love mercy and to walk
humbly with your God?'

For Further Reflection

Micah 6:8

Let nature testify of God

Our Lord has written the promise of the resurrection, not in books alone, but in every leaf in springtime.

Martin Luther

For Further Reflection
Psalm 91:1

Joy comes in the morning

The darkest hour is just before the dawn.
Be encouraged – the sun will shine again.
God won't fail you!

For Further Reflection
Psalm 30:5

Going up yonder

Why should we grieve when our loved ones die?
For we'll meet them again in a cloudless sky;
for Easter is more than a beautiful story,
it's the promise of a life of eternal glory.

♪

For Further Reflection
Revelation 21:4